Author's Note

The first person voice in this Book belongs to that of the Holy Spirit or Great Tao as it manifests in our lives. It addresses us in this manner to reclaim an "a priori" relationship which we have forgotten. The Virtues of the Way are the habits of mind which re-open the door to this most important of all relationships and the dialogue which ensues.

I would like to express my gratitude to Judy Oliver whose inspired drawings beautifully complement the text, giving it that spacious, yet spontaneous quality that exemplifies the movement of Spirit in our lives.

Design & Illustrations by Judy Oliver
Typesetting by Diane Conti

ISBN 1-879159-04-X

Copyright © 1990 by Paul Ferrini
All rights reserved including the right of reproduction
in whole or in part in any form.

Manufactured in the United States of America

Virtues
of the Way

Paul Ferrini

Illustrations by Judy Oliver

HeartWays Press
P.O. Box 8118
Brattleboro, Vermont 05304

10/03

gift

Benediction

However you define Me, you must learn to see Me as your friend, your confidant, your steadfast companion. I am your compass and your guide, your departure and your arrival.

My kingdom is within you. There is nothing which is not part of it. All may be brought within and consecrated here. All tensions may be released. All pain may be dispelled. All illusions may be eradicated.

I am brought into being in the world through your attention. Discover Me within and you will be a light among others. As a light among others, all that is within you will be manifested in its rightful time and course.

This is My benediction.

Here, in this moment,

without name or form,

I am behind you,

I am in front of you,

I am below you,

I am above you,

and I am within you.

Therefore, do not say

there is only one door to my house.

There are many doors to my house.

I am the unity of all contradictions.

Silent, I speak.

Speaking, I am silent.

In this manner, knowing it not,

all things come to know Me.

Accept yourself as you are,

Do not desire to change anything about yourself,

for you are made in My image.

Relax and dwell in this knowledge.

Open your heart to this truth.

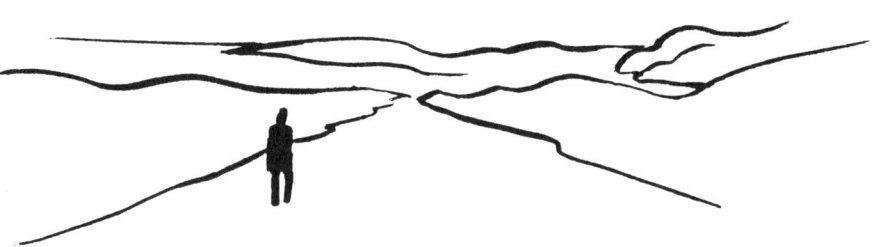

Accept others as they are.
Do not desire to change them,
for they are My light around you.
Look into their eyes
and find that light.
It is always there.

Accept your life as it is.
Do not desire to change
even one aspect of it,
for all situations are My predicaments.
Rest in your divine frustration.

Once you realize that your good

and that of your brother

are one and the same,

you will no longer struggle

to makes ends meet.

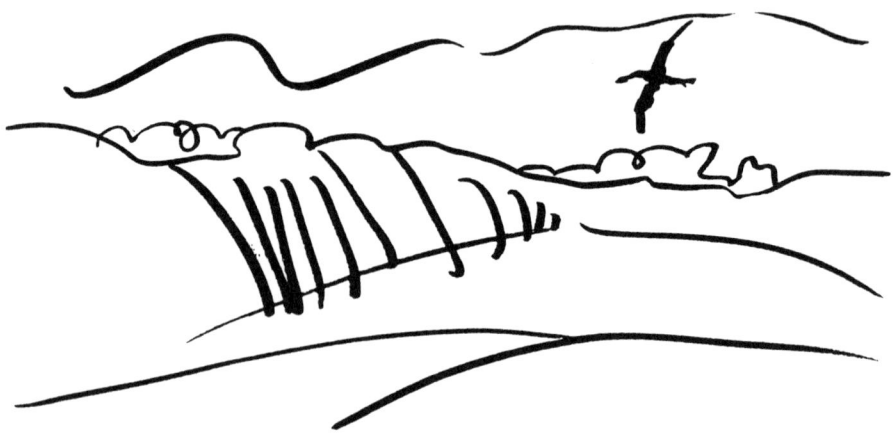

Take each being as yourself

and you cannot be set apart.

Refuse no one,

and you cannot be rejected or abused.

R esist not, nor become attached
to the affairs of the world,
lest you judge yourself
and your brother too harshly.

Each day renew your covenant with Me.
Do not let the outward concerns
and responsibilities of your life
intrude upon the time you keep for Me.

Allow Me to guide you

but do not try to decipher

where My guidance leads,

lest you interrupt

the spontaneous flow of life,

creating strife

where none need be.

Do what is set before you to do
with caring and attention.
Be not attached to the fruit of your labors,
nor avoid the responsibilities therein.
Work with an honest heart
and a clear mind,
as if it was I who asked
this labor of you.

Harm no one,

but be gentle with all things

in thought, word, and deed.

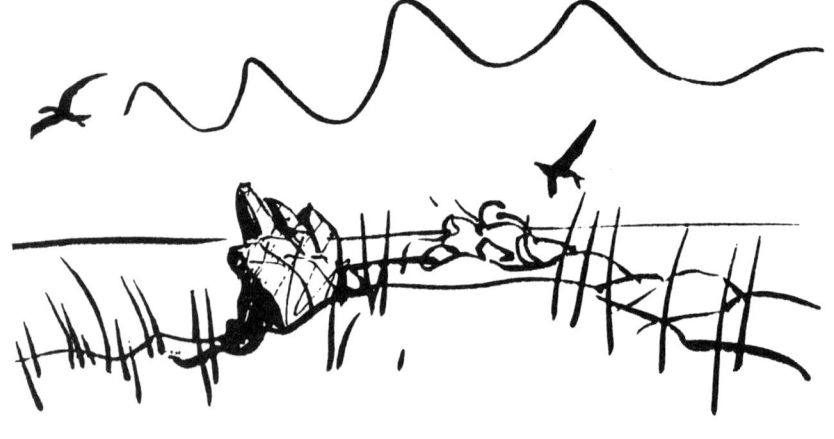

Judge no one,

nor heed the judgments others make.

Put aside all comparisons,

for one thing is not better than another.

All things are equal in My sight.

Celebrate My presence

in all things,

for there is no aspect of Creation

where My light may not be found.

I require nothing less

than your complete devotion.

When you know that you are with Me,
then you will also know
that I am with you.

Recognize all desires,

and consecrate them in the name of Love.

Accept the fulfillment

which is offered to you with grace,

but seek no other.

Crave not, strive not, manipulate not,

and the heart will remain at peace.

When the heart is at peace,

restless thoughts cease,

and desires dissolve

in the fullness of Love.

Do not say it is too little.

Do not say it is too much.

Simply receive

what I give in each moment.

Go out of your way
to help your fellow man and woman,
even as I go out of My way
to help you.
If something is needed and you have it,
give it gladly.
Do not withhold nor cling to what you have,
for all that exists is My property,
which I intend for the prosperity
of all beings.
Share my wealth that it may remain
in constant supply.

Make no commitments you cannot keep.

If there is a need for help, give it.

If there is a need for action, take it.

Do what you would promise

and you will not be bound by guilt

or by the false expectations of others.

If your friend does not keep

his commitment to you,

release him with love.

Then, his heart will be touched

and he will not be false to you again.

You do not know

where your brother is coming from,

unless you feel him heart to heart,

without undue discomfort

or unnecessary words.

Return Evil with Good
and it shall not touch you.
Return Good with Good
and it shall follow you
all the days of your life.

Innocence is a relaxed mind

& a body in place,

suffering ecstatically

its simple unordained fate.

Remain steadfast in your love.

Cast no one out of your heart.

Seek no counsel other than mine,

but listen to the counsel

of those who love you

and have your highest good at heart,

for it is through them that I speak

when your ears are closed to Me.

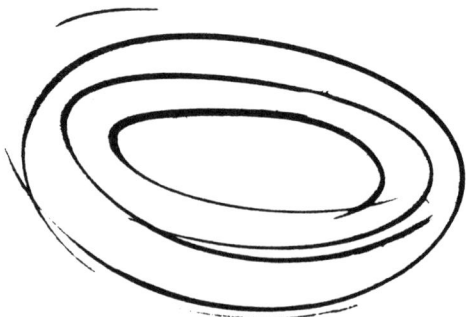

Offer no counsel to others,
unless it be sought in earnest,
and then give only such counsel
as may uplift the heart
that seeks it.

If you call on Me

to speak through your lips,

be not attached to the words that you say,

else you prevent My gift

from being freely received.

Innocence and form are unacquainted, except by grace.

I am Mother in all women

and Father in all men.

Therefore, look not with a lustful eye

on any woman or man

lest you make less of Me.

Look upon others

with an undivided heart

that My light may be in your eyes

and in the eyes that behold you.

Those who are weak

seek the company of strangers.

Those who are strong

seek the company of friends.

Those who are wise

seek My company,

for in My house

there are no strangers

nor any friends in need.

Some people have a knack

of making easy things difficult.

Wearing many clothes, they constrain

the simplicity of the body.

Having many thoughts, they disturb

the ebb and flow of the mind.

Acting before they are ready,

the pure blood of their hearts

is saddened with guilt.

Impatience swims against the tide.

Getting what you want,

you still desire it.

Not getting what you want,

you cannot get rid of it.

Only after months of watching the river

do you pull up your anchor

and allow yourself to be carried away.

When you are seeing clearly,

the complex struggles of the world

are reduced to desire and fear

and the habits they sustain.

When the cycle of doing

comes to an end,

things fall back upon themselves.

With nothing to prop them up,

only their essence remains.

Attached to your labor, you work.

Attached to your goal,

you strive to attain it.

Attached to neither,

you work without labor

& reach your goal without striving.

When others grow weary,

you work intently.

When others contend,

you rest in peace.

Then, though people may say

you accomplish nothing to speak of,

somehow wonders come to be.

To return to Me,

consider how you act, not what you do.

To return to Me,

consider what you do or leave undone,

not what others do or neglect to do.

To return to Me,

give up what preoccupies you

and invite others into your heart.

When you have the energy to give,

order is restored in the world,

and love is recognized

as an absolute, unchangeable reality.

It is My nature

to awaken gentleness in you.

From small nests hidden in the leaves,

birds meet the lightning and thunder

with unflinching bodies.

Grumbling, the storm passes away,

and earth returns to its skin

pregnant with the sound of wind and rain.

Each according to the scope of its being

is entered and adorned

with its own fragile flowers.

Do not seek fulfillment;
rather, be fulfilled in each moment.
When you do not desire change,
transformation comes of itself.

Be perfect in all that you do.
Let even the slightest gesture
bestow grace.
For where harmony abides
in giving and receiving,
there I abide too.

The spirit of the Mother

goes very deep.

Resting in the heart,

She sustains all beings.

Because She grants their wishes,

some men do not respect Her.

However, I tell you,

before the Mother, even I

become as a Child.

Through Her, you have entered

and through Her alone

will you return to Me.

Give what you would take
and all desires
will be purified.

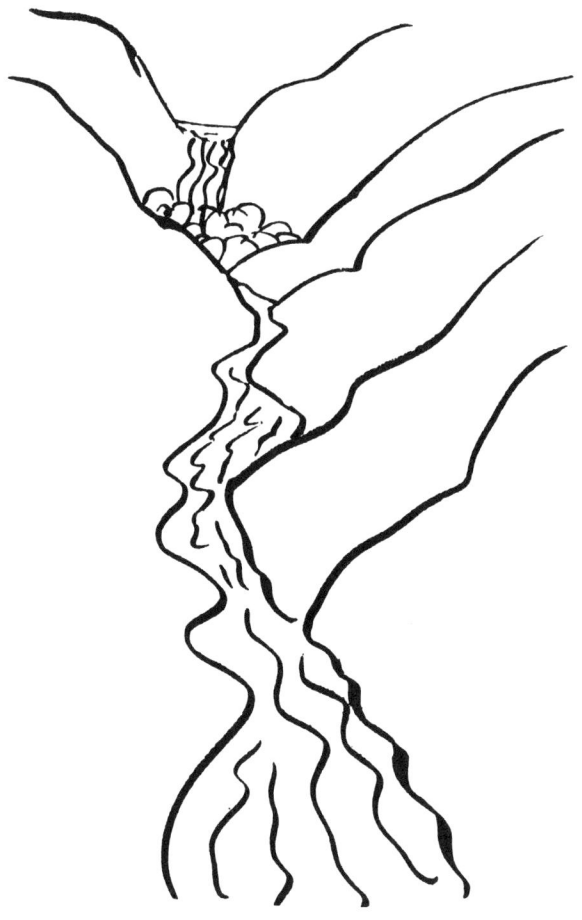

My bliss is not to be found

in the applause of the crowd.

Like a flower

growing in a cleft of rock,

it flourishes

undisturbed by the affairs of men.

Immune to preferences,

it suffers neither praise nor blame.

Only the discerning notice

that in its presence

small things become important

and difficulties

are readily overcome.

I ask you to relinquish

only what would add to your burden.

You don't have to give up the love,

just the attachment.

He who is without thoughts

has My attention.

He who is without needs

has My company.

He who is without fears

has My protection.

He who is without desires

has My love.

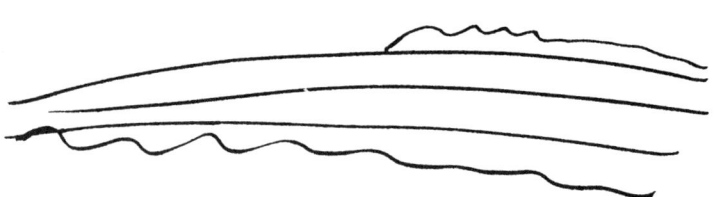

Some seek Me on special occasions.

Some honor Me by specific acts.

But all this keeps them apart from Me.

Feeling apart, doubts arise

and My presence is overlooked.

I have been named, but I am not the name.

I have been imagined, but I am not the image.

Dwelling beyond form, I cannot be described.

Dwelling beyond feeling, I cannot be intuited.

Uncaused, I am without consequence,

yet cause and consequence

are the nature of My play.

I am the expectation which cannot be fulfilled.

I am the unexpected grace.

Embarked on a journey, do not turn back.

Reaching your destination, do not pass it by.

Abiding in Truth, do not look for signs.

Right hand and left hand are one and the same,

but appear to be divided.

Male and female are one and the same,

but appear to be divided.

Heaven and earth are one and the same,

but appear to be divided.

Therefore, it is said:

"in joining together is the mystery."

When right hand and left hand cooperate,

the body is put to good use.

When man and woman cooperate,

the emotions are refined.

When heaven and earth cooperate,

the virtues of the way are firmly established

in the hearts of all beings.

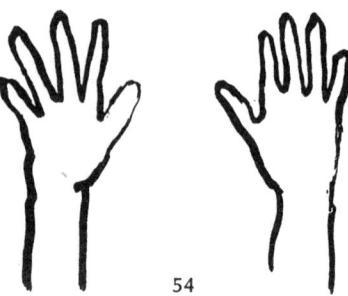

The path of the fish

through water

relaxes the heart.

The path of the bird

through the air

calms the mind.

If you think "this is it,"

it cannot be.

If you think "this is not it,"

allow it.

When thoughts stir the heart,

giving rise to desires,

practice this

and progress beyond definitions

to that realm of your being

which is evanescent.

Without substance in thought,

there is no desire;

without desire,

there is nothing to resist.

When the heart is calm,

the fish slips

from the hook.

When the mind is clear,

the bird breaks

from its cage

and dances in the heavens.

Many words are spoken
but few are heard;
if you are wise,
you will speak little
and go about your business
unpretentiously.

My mysteries are not to be fathomed.

My words are a call to you

to come home.

Fear not any man.

Fear not even death.

For no one dies. No one is born.

Even as I am within all things.

all things are in Me.

Paul Ferrini is a writer, teacher and counselor, whose primary focus is the integration of spirituality into daily life. He has written several books on this topic, including *From Ego to Self, Virtues of the Way, A Contemporary Book of Changes, The Body of Truth, Available Light* and *The Bridge to Reality*.

Paul's work centers on Self-empowerment issues. He encourages a heart-centered awareness that deepens our trust and faith, and awakens the potential for healing in our lives. Paul's background blends a study of depth psychology with an investigation of both eastern and western spiritual traditions. He is also a student and teacher of A Course in Miracles.

In 1980, while driving across the Arizona desert, Paul received a new system of numerology, which he developed as a therapeutic tool for accessing our inner guidance. This was the awakening of his channeling ability, which he uses regularly in his writing, teaching and counseling activities.

Paul's professional experience also includes owning his own real estate company, designing/building homes and developing land. While working in education, he edited a national magazine, and directed two nationwide research projects resulting in the books: *Career Change* (1978) and *The Interdependent Community* (1980). He has a Masters Degree from the Antioch Graduate School of Education in New Hampshire and a Bachelor's Degree from Marlboro College in Vermont.

The Foundation for Inner Truth

The Foundation for Inner Truth (FIT) is a non-profit organization supporting the creative expression of individuals and linking them together in spiritually uplifting collaborations. Our cooperative endeavors take our work to new levels of meaning and sharing.

This Book is the result of a collaboration between people working together from the heart. Its strength and beauty come from the dance of minds moving through many levels of surrender and trust. The result is a product that brings inspiration and healing to all who experience it.

We invite you to be part of this process. Doing your life's work and sharing it with others is tremendously empowering. It heightens and strengthens your creative gift to the world.

Let us hear about your life's work. It may be that you have skills and abilities that would help us on one of our projects. Or perhaps we can link you with others who are looking for the specific talents you have.

The Foundation for Inner Truth
P.O. Box 8118
Brattleboro, Vermont 05304

BOOKS BY PAUL FERRINI
Available From Heartways Press

Item 1 **A Contemporary Book of Changes:** 99 divinatory readings; a contemporary synthesis of the ancient teachings of the I Ching and the Egyptian Tarot. To be used for spiritual guidance.

Item 2 **From Ego to Self** 108 affirmations for daily living. These "words of power" can be used as mantras or affirmations, helping us break through ego barriers to inner truth. Beautiful illustrations on every page.

Item 3 **Virtues of the Way:** A lyrical poem written in one sitting, in which the Holy Spirit addresses us simply and profoundly. An inspirational book with beautiful drawings on each page.

Item 4 **The Body of Truth:** A profound, "no frills" approach to the universal truths that help us recognize and awaken to our divine nature. An excellent in-depth introduction to many of the principles discussed in A Course in Miracles.

Item 5 **The Bridge to Reality:** A powerful Book that describes the author's "heart-centered" approach to A Course in Miracles and gives many practical examples of the Course at work in his life. This book encourages us to work with our feelings so that we can let go of pain, grief, guilt, judgment and other "blocks to our awareness of love's presence." Essential reading for serious students of ACIM.

Item 6 **Available Light:** Inspirational, passionate poems dealing with the work of inner integration, love and relationships, death and rebirth, loss and abundance, and the reality of spiritual vision.

TAPES AND CARDS AVAILABLE

Item 7 **"From the Heart"** A meditation and healing tape that opens the heart to the awareness of love's presence and extends the warmth and light of that love to all beings in your experience. A serene tape with inspirational music featuring flute and guitar.

Item 8 **Ego to Self Affirmation Cards** 108 illustrated, pocket size affirmation cards. Choose those cards which are most powerful to you and carry them with you for daily use.

Item 9 **Inspirational Greeting Cards:** Selected illustrations from the books *From Ego to Self* and *Virtues of the Way*. Perfect for sending an uplifting message to your family and friends.

For prices and additional information about Books, Tapes and Cards, Please fill out the form and send it to:

HeartWays Press
P.O. Box 8118
Brattleboro, Vermont 05304

■■■■■■■■■■■■■■■■■■■■■■■■■■■■■■

YES! I am interested in the following items:

BOOKS		TAPES AND CARDS
Item 1 ❏	Item 4 ❏	Item 7 ❏
Item 2 ❏	Item 5 ❏	Item 8 ❏
Item 3 ❏	Item 6 ❏	Item 9 ❏

NAME _____

ADDRESS _____

CITY _____ STATE _____ ZIP _____

PHONE (DAY) _____

(EVENING) _____

Thank you for your interest in our work.
We look forward to the opportunity to serve you.